The Teen Guide to Adulting:
Gaining Financial Independence

What You Need to Know About

TAXES

CORONA BREZINA

Rosen
YA
™

New York

Published in 2021 by The Rosen Publishing Group, Inc.
29 East 21st Street, New York, NY 10010

First Edition

Library of Congress Cataloging-in-Publication Data

Names: Brezina, Corona, author.
Title: What you need to know about taxes / Corona Brezina.
Description: First edition. | New York: Rosen Publishing, 2021. | Series: The teen guide to adulting:
gaining financial independence | Includes bibliographical references and index.
Identifiers: LCCN 2019016082| ISBN 9781725340725 (library bound) | ISBN 9781725340718 (pbk.)
Subjects: LCSH: Taxation—United States—Juvenile literature. | Income tax—United States—
Juvenile literature.
Classification: LCC HJ2381 .B725 2021 | DDC 336.200973—dc23
LC record available at https://lccn.loc.gov/2019016082

Manufactured in China

CONTENTS

INTRODUCTION

For many teens, getting a summer or after-school job is a rite of passage. Receiving a first paycheck is another landmark moment. Earning your own pay represents a degree of financial freedom, as well as a new responsibility to make sound decisions concerning your money.

If you examine your pay stub closely, though, you will probably observe another reality of adulthood: taxes. Payroll taxes and income taxes are deducted from employees' paychecks. The amount of your earnings that you take home is reduced by a few percentage points. When tax returns are due in April, you may be required to file an income tax return, depending on how much money you earned in the past year.

It's important for young adults to understand how taxes work to attain financial security. To begin with, Americans pay many different kinds of taxes in addition to income taxes. Some are easy to recognize, such as the sales tax on receipts or the payment due on property taxes. Others, such as excise taxes on specific goods or tariffs on imports, may increase the price tag even though you may not realize that a tax contributed to some of the cost.

All of these taxes pay for services for the public. Taxes fund the military and national parks. They pay for schools, scientific research, health care for retirees, and infrastructure such as roads and sanitation systems. Taxes are used to provide

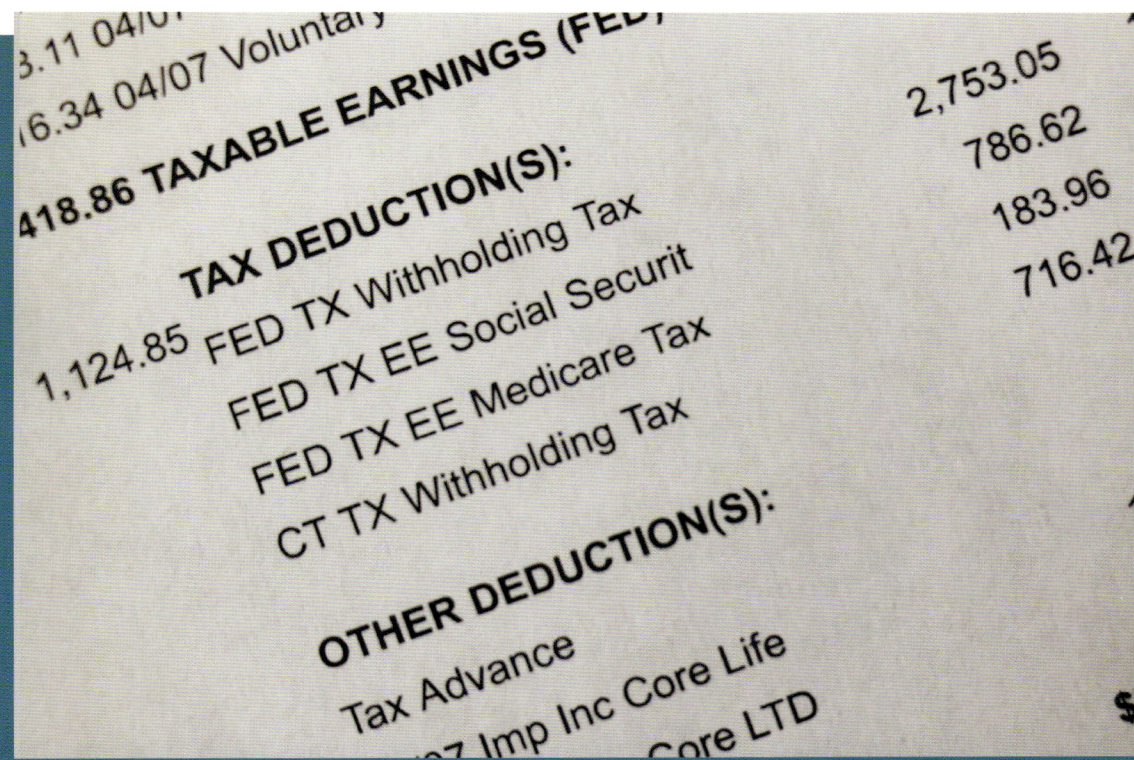

3.11 04/0
6.34 04/07 Voluntary
418.86 TAXABLE EARNINGS (FED
2,753.05
786.62
183.96
716.42

TAX DEDUCTION(S):

1,124.85 FED TX Withholding Tax
FED TX EE Social Securit
FED TX EE Medicare Tax
CT TX Withholding Tax

OTHER DEDUCTION(S):

Tax Advance
Imp Inc Core Life
Core LTD

$

The government collects taxes to pay for public services, including safety net programs such as Social Security and Medicare that help the poor, elderly, and disabled.

essential services that require a reliable source of revenue. If the government did not provide these services, low-income families might not be able to afford quality education and cities might not be able to pay for policing.

Taxing and spending requires balancing priorities. Legislators have to weigh whether it's better to keep taxes low so that people have more money to contribute to economic growth or to collect more taxes to provide quality services to a greater number of people. They also have to decide which types of taxes to draw on for revenue and which programs to prioritize. Tax policy is a complex area that can affect the health of the economy and the lives of individuals.

Taxes are a daunting subject that many people prefer to avoid. It's easy to complain about high taxes and take for granted the services paid for by taxes. But all Americans should understand the laws and procedures related to the taxes they're required to pay, as well as the significance of the tax decisions made by lawmakers.

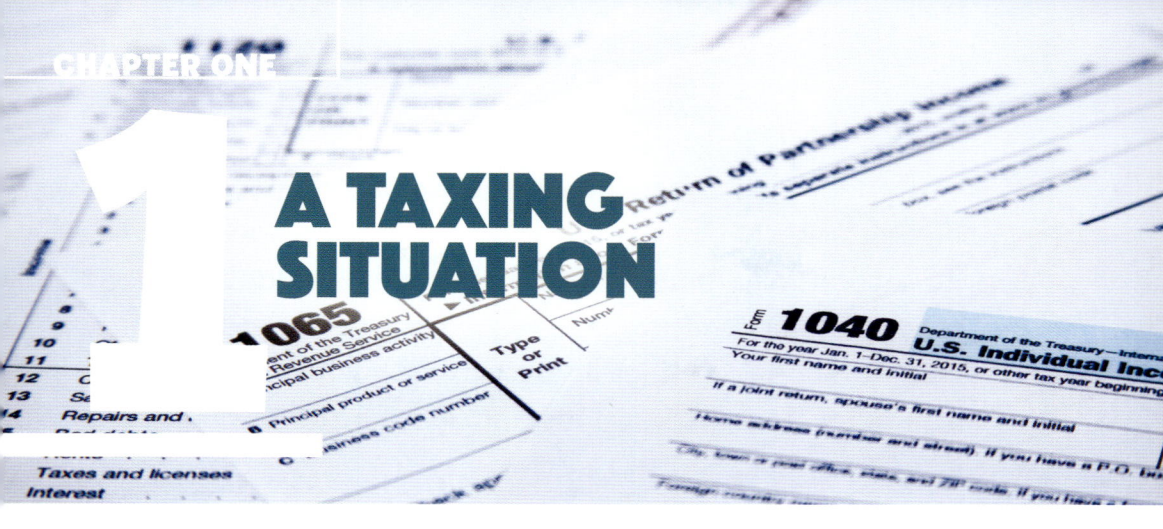

CHAPTER ONE

A TAXING SITUATION

The Internal Revenue Service (IRS) defines taxes as "required payments of money to governments that are used to provide public goods and services for the benefit of the community as a whole." Most taxpayers hate paying taxes, and part of the reason is that they're required, or involuntary. People would prefer to choose how they spend their own money, and it might seem that giving it up to taxes relinquishes any control about where the money goes. But decisions about taxation and spending are made by elected officials. Most taxpayers are also citizens who can vote for representatives who they believe will make wise fiscal decisions.

THE TAX CODE

The tax code—officially known as the Internal Revenue Code—is written by the US Congress. It constitutes Title 26 of the United States Code, which is a collection of all of the laws enacted by Congress. The first US Code was published in 1926, although codification of tax laws dates back to 1874.

The tax code is organized into ten subtitles covering different aspects of taxation, and the subtitles are divided into sections. The types of taxes addressed include income taxes, estate and gift taxes, employment taxes, and excise taxes. Additional subtitles address topics such as procedure and administration, trust funds, and financing of presidential election campaigns.

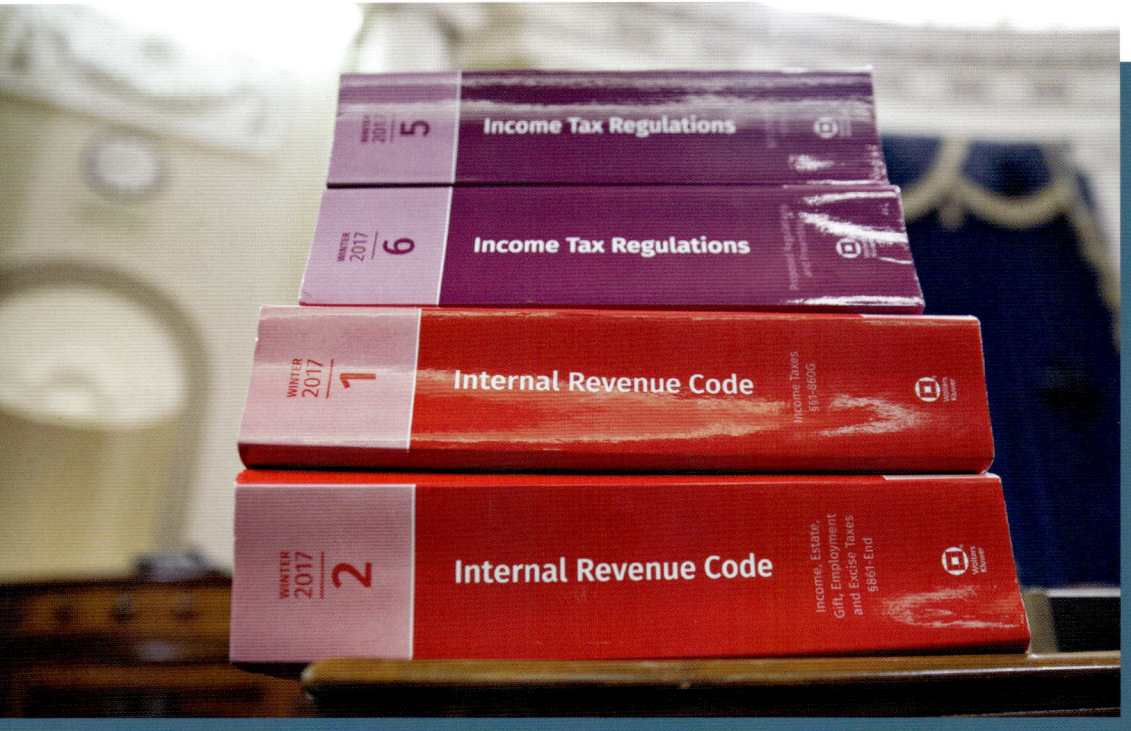

Federal tax laws are found in the Internal Revenue Code. *Tax professionals also consult the* Income Tax Regulations *reference, which provides interpretations of the tax laws.*

The IRS, a branch of the US Department of Treasury, is charged with carrying out these duties described in the tax code. The IRS collects taxes and issues refunds and credits. It also enforces tax regulations issued by the Treasury, which are the official interpretation of the provisions in the tax code. The IRS enforces revenue rulings as well, which are the agency's own interpretation of the tax code and other relevant laws.

The Internal Revenue Service Building in Washington, DC, serves as the headquarters of the IRS, the agency that administers and enforces federal tax laws in the United States.

The tax code has been the subject of much criticism by commentators from all different political leanings. Most critics agree that the tax code—which is divided into fifty-three titles and contains nearly ten thousand different sections—is too long and bloated. They claim that it gives preferential treatment to some groups and contains too many loopholes that allow people to avoid certain taxes. Some politicians have even proposed abolishing the tax code and devising a new tax system. Most critics instead support simplifying and clarifying the existing tax code, and the government has periodically passed new legislation revising tax laws.

TYPES OF TAXES

Just as there are different levels of government—federal, state, and local—each level raises revenue and spends it on services for residents. Most federal revenue comes from taxation and contributions to programs such as Social Security and Medicare. State and local governments collect taxes, too, but they also receive money through intergovernmental transfers. The federal government transfers money to the states, and state governments transfer money to local governments. Intergovernmental transfers account for about a third of state revenue and two-fifths of local revenue, according to the Tax Policy Center. In total, taxes collected on state and local levels are much lower than federal taxes. For example, out of about $5.3 trillion in government revenue in 2016, about 65 percent of taxes were federal, 20 percent state, and 15 percent local.

The federal government relies mainly on income taxes for revenue, followed by payroll taxes (which pay for social programs) and corporate income taxes. State and local governments tend to rely more heavily on property taxes and sales taxes as well as income taxes.

There are various approaches to assessing taxes, which are all seen in the many different taxes collected on federal, state, and

Taxes are levied by different levels of the government, which pays for services provided to the public by federal, state, county, and local agencies.

local levels. Tax systems can be categorized according to which taxpayers bear the greatest tax burden. Under a progressive tax system, the rich pay higher tax rates than the poor. The federal income tax is a progressive tax. Earners with higher incomes pay higher tax rates than low-income taxpayers. Under a regressive tax system, the poor pay higher tax rates than the rich. The payroll tax that funds Social Security is a regressive system. In 2019, earners paid a rate of 7.65 percent on earnings up

THE TAX CUTS AND JOBS ACT OF 2017

In late 2017, President Donald Trump signed the Tax Cuts and Jobs Act (TCJA), the most significant revision to the tax code since the 1980s. The law dramatically reduced corporate income taxes and created a substantial new deduction that applies to some businesses. It slightly reduced income tax rates for individual taxpayers. The law also increased the exemption for estate taxes and for the alternative minimum tax (AMT), meaning that wealthy taxpayers who are subject to these taxes will owe less. The reductions for corporations are permanent, but changes to individual rates will expire in 2025.

The act also aimed to simplify income tax returns. According to Accounting Today, however, the changes did not succeed in simplifying the process of filing personal income tax returns.

Initial reaction to the TCJA was mixed. Some analysts predicted that the act would boost the economy and help create jobs. Critics claimed that its provisions favored the wealthy and would create budget deficits by collecting less tax revenue. The full economic impact of the TCJA will not be known until the new rates have been in place for a few years.

to $132,900, according to the Social Security Administration. Therefore, wealthy earners pay an overall lower rate than people earning under $132,900. Under a proportional tax system, also known as a flat tax, all income groups pay the same rate. A proportional tax tends to place a greater burden on low-income earners, however, because the poor are more likely to be unable to afford to pay a set percentage of their income than the rich. Some states assess income taxes using a proportional tax system.

Consumption taxes are imposed depending on the amount of money people spend rather than the amount they earn. Sales taxes, for example, are a consumption tax.

TAKING IN TAXES

In 2017, the federal government took in $3.3 trillion in revenue, according to the Center on Budget and Policy Priorities. The largest portion came from income taxes, which made up 48 percent of tax revenue. The next largest source was payroll taxes, which funds Social Security and other social programs, making up 35 percent of revenue. Corporate income taxes made up 9 percent of revenue, and other taxes, such as excise and estate taxes, made up 8 percent of the total revenue.

The federal government spent $4 trillion in 2017, according to the Center on Budget and Policy Priorities. The largest proportion of spending went to Social Security, which pays retirement benefits to retired workers and other eligible recipients. Social Security accounted for 24 percent of spending. Medicare, the Children's Health Insurance Program, and other health care programs accounted for 26 percent of federal spending. Defense and international security programs accounted for 15 percent of the budget. About 9 percent of spending went to social programs such as the Supplemental Nutrition Assistance Program (SNAP), child care assistance, and help for paying energy bills. Eight percent went toward benefits for veterans, and 7 percent paid for interest on the federal debt. Education, transportation infrastructure, and science and medical research combined accounted for 7 percent of spending.

In total, the federal government spent more money in 2017 than it took in through revenue. The government borrowed $665 billion to fully fund all programs. When spending is larger than revenue, the difference is called the budget deficit. (When spending is equal to revenue, the budget is said to be balanced.) The government has been running a budget deficit for most years since 1970. The total of the budget deficits is called the national debt. Investors buy shares of the national debt and receive interest payments in return. That's why 7 percent of federal spending in 2017 went toward interest on the national debt.

State governments collected about $951 billion in tax revenue, according to the Census Bureau 2017 Annual Survey of State Tax Collections. At $156 billion, California took in the most revenue. Wyoming, by contrast, had the smallest revenue, at $1.6 billion. The largest source of tax revenues overall for states were sales and gross receipts taxes, at $453 billion, followed by state income taxes, at $398 billion. (A gross receipts tax, which is only collected in a few states, is

14,433,737,989,712

YOUR *Family share* 122,303

THE NATIONAL DEBT CLOCK

e Service

New York City's National Debt Clock, shown here in 2011, displays the current national debt of the United States. The number increases when the federal government runs a budget deficit.

levied on some or all goods and services sold by a business.) Other state taxes included license taxes and property taxes. Local governments tend to rely on property taxes as their largest source of revenue.

State and local governments can run deficits and accumulate debt, although most bring in enough revenue to meet expenses. Some states even run surpluses, collecting more revenue than necessary. Alaska, for example, has accumulated a surplus of 140 percent since 2003, according to Watchdog.org. Other states run long-term deficits that threaten economic performance. New Jersey and Illinois in particular have experienced significant shortfalls every year since the early 2000s.

CHAPTER TWO

THE TAXES AMERICANS PAY

Americans often associate the word "taxes" with filing their annual income tax return. However, Americans are also taxed on the money they earn through payroll and income taxes and on the money they spend through sales taxes. The prices of some goods and services might already have been increased due to excise taxes paid through a distributor or producer. Prices of imported goods might reflect tariffs paid upon bringing them into the country. One of the oldest taxes in the United States, the estate tax, is imposed on very few Americans in the twenty-first century.

PAYROLL TAX

If you look at the stub from your paycheck, you may observe certain deductions. One component of the amount taken out of your earnings is Federal Insurance Contributions Act (FICA) tax. Your paycheck may specify that your payroll tax, as it's called, contributes to both Social Security and Medicare.

Employees pay 6.2 percent for Social Security and 1.45 percent for Medicare out of their paychecks, and the amount is matched by their employers, for a total that is equivalent to 15.3 percent of the employee's pay, according to the Social Security Administration. The Social Security portion is not collected on income over $132,900—a wage base limit. Medicare has no such limit, and earners who make over $200,000 a year must pay an additional 0.9 percent on excess income. The employer does not match the Additional Medicare Tax.

The Social Security tax pays for two programs: Old Age Survivors Insurance (OASI) and Disability Insurance (DI). The money you pay into Social Security is not held for your own use upon retirement. Rather, it pays for the benefits of current recipients. Social Security payroll taxes are put into a Social Security trust fund that cannot be used for any other purpose. The Medicare portion of payroll taxes is deposited into a Medicare trust fund, and it pays for health care benefits for retirees and people with disabilities.

According to some economic forecasts, Social Security and Medicare are both in danger of running out of money within the next couple decades. The amount of money being paid by taxpayers will not meet the costs of the programs. For the programs to remain financially sound, taxpayer contributions will have to increase or benefits will have to be cut.

Taxpayers who are self-employed do not have their contributions matched by an employer. Therefore, they are required to pay both their portion and the employer's share.

Many Americans over the age of sixty-five receive health care through Medicare, which is funded by payroll taxes paid by employees, employers, and self-employed individuals.

This rate—double that of regular employees—is called the self-employment tax. It was enacted by the Self-Employment Contributions Act (SECA) in 1954.

CORPORATE INCOME TAXES

Although businesses and corporations pay what is called an income tax, the tax is actually levied on their profits. And the taxes imposed on a company depend on how it is incorporated. Corporations known as pass-through businesses do not pay corporate income tax, instead passing the tax burden on to individual owners to be taxed as personal income. For companies called C corporations, the corporate income tax rate in 2019 was 21 percent, the lowest rate since 1939, as reported by The Balance. The 2017 Tax Cuts and Jobs Act reduced the rate from 35 percent. But most corporations were able to find tax loopholes. They had paid an effective rate of only 18.6 percent, according to The Balance.

Corporations are allowed to deduct the cost of business expenses from the profits that are taxed. These business expenses include the cost of goods sold, employees' pay, advertising, the cost of some equipment, interest (such as on loans), travel, and operating expenses.

Big corporations are able to claim deductions and exploit tax laws to reduce their corporate income taxes. Every year, there are news stories about highly profitable companies that manage to pay no corporate income tax and even receive rebates. In 2019, for example, it was reported by CBS that

Amazon.com employees pack shipments at a distribution center. Despite earning billions annually in profits, the company paid no federal taxes in 2019.

Amazon, Netflix, and General Motors avoided paying corporate income taxes.

EXCISE TAXES

Excise taxes are similar to sales taxes—they constitute a percentage of the cost paid. Most excise taxes are paid by the manufacturer or wholesaler, which passes the cost down to the consumer in the final price. Unlike sales tax, which is a consumption tax imposed on a broad range of purchases, excise

THE REAGAN TAX CUTS

In 1980, Ronald Reagan ran for president during a period of economic turmoil with the campaign promise that he would revive the economy by cutting taxes. After winning the election, he carried through when he signed the Economic Recovery Tax Act of 1981, which put into effect some of the biggest tax cuts in US history. The wealthy saw the greatest benefits, with the highest income tax rates decreasing from 70 to 50 percent; rates for lower earners fell from 14 to 11 percent, according to a Medium article titled "OTD in History ... August 13, 1981, President Ronald Reagan Signs Biggest Tax Cuts into Law." The act triggered a drastic increase in interest rates and caused the national debt to soar. After winning reelection in 1984, Reagan signed the Tax Reform Act of 1986, which lowered the highest income tax rate to 28 percent (according to Bloomberg), slashed corporate taxes, and simplified the tax code. The revenue losses caused by the Reagan tax cuts were partially offset by tax increases implemented in 1982, 1983, 1984, 1987, 1990, and 1993.

taxes are imposed on specific goods, services, and activities. The four largest sources of federal excise revenue are highway-related revenue, aviation-related revenue, alcohol, and tobacco. Some excise taxes are referred to as sin taxes because they are imposed on products and services considered unhealthy, which can be used to justify the increased cost imposed by high excise taxes. In 2010, for example, a 10 percent excise tax was imposed on indoor tanning, which is a dangerous practice that can contribute to cancer, according to medical professionals.

A less common form of excise tax is the so-called luxury tax levied on nonessential goods and services.

Some excise taxes are put in trust funds intended for a specific purpose. The largest amount of federal excise taxes come from highway-related sources. Taxes on gasoline and diesel fuel bring in the greatest revenue, but taxes are also imposed on highway use by trucks and the purchase of goods

Some state and local governments tax sugary drinks such as soda, a measure often intended to discourage consumption and pay for programs related to health and wellness.

such as trucks or trailers. The revenue goes into the Highway Trust Fund. Similarly, excise taxes related to aviation—mostly imposed on passenger tickets—goes into the Airport and Airway Trust Fund. Revenue from excise taxes on alcohol and tobacco are put into a general fund.

CUSTOM DUTIES

Custom duties, also called tariffs, are imposed on goods imported into one country from another. Tariffs are paid by the person bringing the foreign merchandise into the country. If a retailer sells goods from China, for example, any custom duties are paid by the retailer, not the Chinese producer. Americans returning from international travel may have to pay custom duties on items purchased abroad, above a certain exemption.

Tariffs bring in federal revenue, but they can also be used as a tool for economic policy. Protectionism is the practice of restricting imports to protect domestic producers from trade competition. High tariffs are generally passed down to buyers, making prices of imported goods higher. If a government imposes high tariffs on another country's goods, the other country's government may retaliate with its own tariffs, leading to a trade war. In 2018, the Trump administration imposed a broad range of tariffs on steel, aluminum, and other Chinese imports. Some tax experts, including analysts at the Tax Foundation, concluded that the tariffs ultimately hurt middle- and low-income Americans and damaged the country's economic performance.

A freighter from China is stacked with cargo in a Florida harbor. Imposing tariffs on imported goods increases the prices paid by consumers.

ESTATE TAXES AND GIFT TAXES

The IRS describes the federal estate tax as "a tax on your right to transfer property at your death" to heirs. The value of the estate, above a certain exemption, is taxed at a rate of 40 percent. Only the very wealthy are subject to federal estate taxes. According to the Center on Budget and Policy Priorities, only one in one thousand estates are affected by estate taxes. In 2017, the exemption was set at $11.2 million per person, set to increase through 2025 due to inflation. Estates left to spouses are not taxed.

An estate tax may be levied on property that is transferred from a deceased person to their heirs. This can include money, real estate, stocks, business interests, and other assets.

A federal gift tax is an excise tax imposed on gifts, paid by the person giving the gift. It was originally created to prevent the wealthy from avoiding estate taxes by passing their estates on during their lifetimes. A gift tax must be paid on gifts over $15,000 per person in 2019, with a lifetime exemption of $11.4 million on taxable gifts, according to NerdWallet. Gifts under $15,000 do not count toward the lifetime exemption, and gifts to a spouse are not taxed. Tax rates range from 18 percent to 40 percent.

MYTHS & FACTS

MYTH You don't have to pay income taxes on tips or on income from side jobs.

Fact The IRS considers tips from jobs at workplaces such as restaurants and hotels to be taxable income. If you earn more than $20 in a month from tips, you must report and pay payroll and income taxes on the income. If you earn more than $400 from a side job, such as working as a driver for a ride-sharing service, the IRS considers you to be self-employed. You must pay income tax and self-employment tax even if the job isn't your primary source of income.

MYTH If I get a raise, I might be in danger of a huge tax increase by being bumped into a higher tax bracket.

Fact If your income qualifies you for a higher tax rate, only the income exceeding the threshold for the higher rate will be taxed at that rate. The rest of your income will be taxed at applicable rates for each lower tax bracket.

MYTH My tax return is guaranteed to be in good hands if I hire a professional tax preparer.

Fact It's true that most tax preparers are well qualified and perform excellent work preparing returns. They generally provide assistance if you're audited as well. But the IRS recommends checking your tax preparer's credentials and experience. (The IRS website includes a page, "Things to Remember When Choosing a Tax Preparer," that offers tips in selecting a preparer. The IRS also offers the searchable Directory of Federal Tax Return Preparers with Credentials and Select Qualifications on its website.) In particular, stay away from "fly-by-night" or "ghost" preparers, who open up services around tax season and often scam taxpayers.

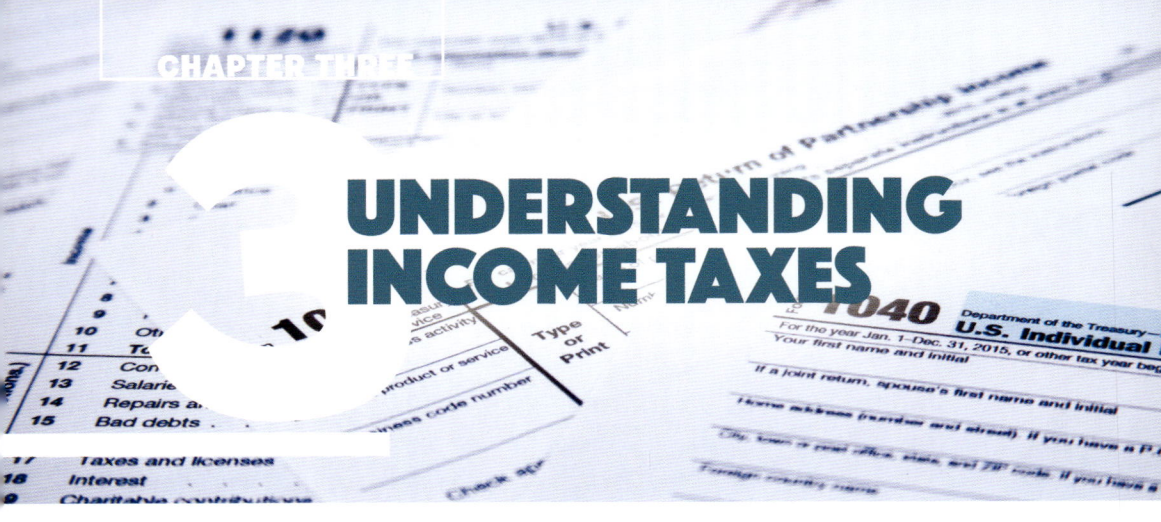

CHAPTER THREE

UNDERSTANDING INCOME TAXES

Federal income taxes are the US government's largest source of revenue. In 2016, Americans paid $1.4 trillion in income taxes, according to statistics released by the IRS in the autumn of 2018. A total of 140.9 million taxpayers earned $10.2 trillion in adjusted gross income. (A person's adjusted gross income is his or her total income minus certain tax-deductible expenses, such as student loan interest or contributions to retirement plans.)

Income tax is a progressive tax—higher earners pay higher rates than lower earners. The proportion of income to taxes paid is very different for top earners versus bottom earners.

In 2016, the top 1 percent of filers earned about 19.7 percent of reported income. The top 10 percent earned about 46.56 percent. The bottom 50 percent of filers earned about 11.6 percent of all reported income.

The top 1 percent paid 37.3 percent of all income taxes collected by the IRS, and the top 10 percent paid 69.47 percent. The top 0.001 percent of taxpayers—about 1,400 very wealthy individuals—paid 3.25 percent of all income taxes. The bottom 50 percent paid a total of 3 percent of all income taxes.

The tax rate for the top 1 percent of earners was an average of 26.9 percent in 2016, according to IRS statistics. Rates for the top 50 percent of earners was 15.9 percent. The bottom 50 percent paid a 3.7 percent rate. Overall, rates rose slightly over the previous ten years. In 2006, the top 10 percent of earners paid 22.8 percent and the top 50 percent of earners 14.1 percent.

The rates for top earners and their share of the tax burden may seem dramatically high compared to lower earners. Historically, however, tax rates have been much steeper for wealthy Americans at various points during the twentieth century.

2019 Individual Income Tax Rates	Single-Taxable Income	Married Filing Jointly-Taxable Income	Head of Household-Taxable Income
10 percent	0 to $ 9,700	0 to $19,400	0 to $13,850
12 percent	$9,701 to $39,475	$19,401 to $78,950	$13,851 to $52,850
22 percent	$39,476 to $84,200	$78,951 to $168,400	$52,851 to $84,200
24 percent	$84,201 to $160,725	$168,401 to $321,450	$84,201 to $160,700
32 percent	$160,726 to $204,100	$321,451 to $408,200	$160,701 to $204,100
35 percent	$204,101 to $510,300	$408,201 to $612,350	$204,101 to $510,300
37 percent	$510,301 and up	$612,351 and up	$510,301 and up

A chart of tax brackets shows that income tax is a progressive tax. Tax brackets indicate the rate a taxpayer will pay for each portion of his or her income.

INCOME TAXES AND US HISTORY

Until the nineteenth century, excise taxes were the primary source of federal tax revenue in the United States. In 1861, the government looked for new sources of funds to pay for the Civil War (1861–1865). Congress passed a Revenue Act that imposed a flat tax of 3 percent on incomes over $800, according to the National Constitution Center. When the money brought in by the measure was inadequate to fund the war, a second Revenue Act established a progressive system in 1862. People earning over $600 would pay 3 percent while those earning more than $10,000 would pay 5 percent. An Office of the Commissioner of Internal Revenue was created in 1862 to collect taxes.

The income tax was repealed in 1872. In 1894, the government once again established an income tax, but it was struck down by the US Supreme Court as unconstitutional because it did not take state population into consideration.

In 1913, the Sixteenth Amendment to the Constitution was ratified, giving the government the right to collect income taxes without regard to state population. That year, the government began taxing incomes over $3,000 at a rate of 1 percent, increasing to 7 percent for incomes over $500,000, according to the IRS. Income taxes were raised in 1916, and when the United States entered World War I in 1917, the War Revenue Act drastically hiked income taxes. By 1918, the highest earners were paying tax rates of 77 percent.

Tax rates decreased again after the war ended in 1918, but the economy was subsequently devastated by the Great Depression, which lasted from 1929 to 1939. The government again raised income taxes, especially on the wealthy, to increase revenue. Taxes continued to rise when the United States entered World War II in 1941. The highest tax rate of 94 percent was imposed on people earning over $200,000, according to The Balance. Even the lowest earners, people making $500 or less annually, had to pay an income tax rate of 23 percent.

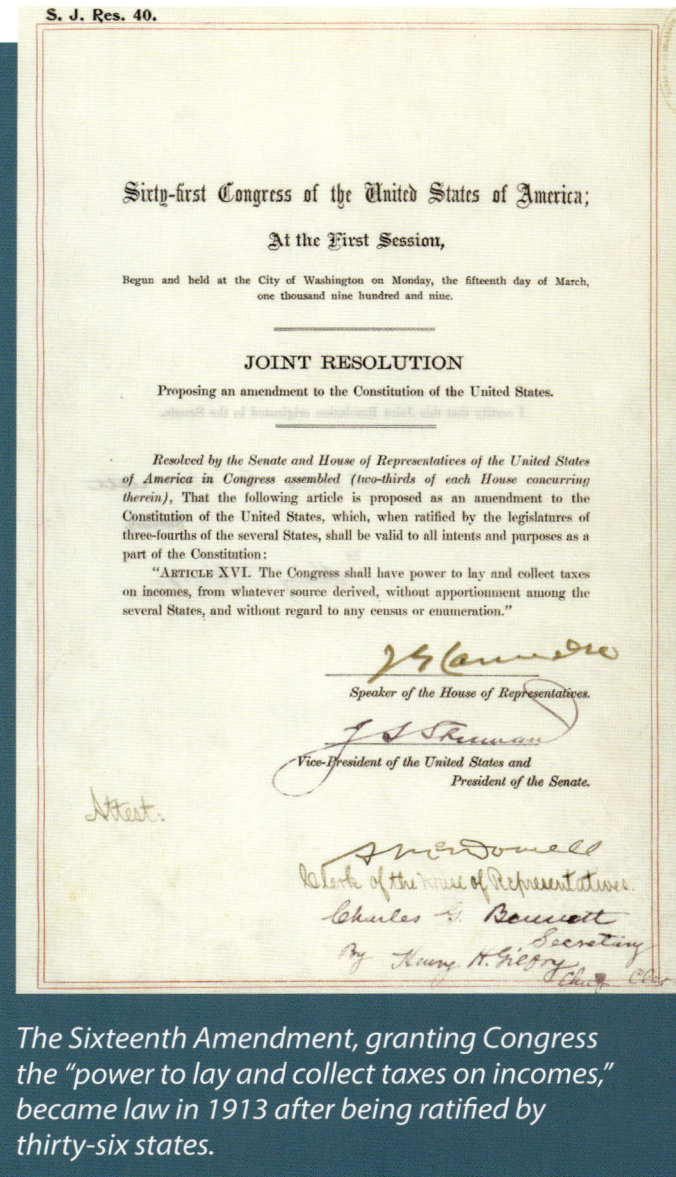

The Sixteenth Amendment, granting Congress the "power to lay and collect taxes on incomes," became law in 1913 after being ratified by thirty-six states.

President Barack Obama signs the Middle Class Tax Relief and Job Creation Act, which includes an extension of a payroll tax cut, on February 22, 2012.

During this period, the government required employers to start withholding taxes, and it introduced quarterly tax payments. Various categories of deductions were introduced as well.

In the 1950s, the Bureau of Internal Revenue was reorganized and renamed the Internal Revenue Service (IRS). The highest tax rate remained at 87 percent after the war. In the 1970s, it was lowered to 70 percent. The tax cuts of the 1980s saw income taxes significantly reduced.

In 1998, the IRS Restructuring and Reform Act modernized the IRS. The agency was charged with improving customer service, reorganizing its structure, and improving technology, such as computer systems and electronic filing for taxpayers.

Tax legislation of the 2000s made changes to tax rules and provided tax relief to Americans. This legislation included the Economic Growth and Tax Relief Reconciliation Act of 2001,

REFUSING TO PAY

For most Americans, paying taxes is an unwelcome yet routine responsibility. For others, refusing to pay taxes is a political act.

In Colonial America, taxation of goods such as tea, sugar, and stamps by the British led to acts of resistance such as the Boston Tea Party and the slogan "No taxation without representation." This citizen rebellion against taxes perceived as unjust helped ignite the American Revolution.

One form of modern tax resistance is a refusal to pay taxes because of political convictions, especially an opposition to war. War tax resisters object to taxation that funds wars or the military. Some resisters refuse to pay any taxes; others withhold only the proportion that would pay for military spending. War tax resistance reached its height during the Vietnam War, but war tax resisters also protested conflicts such as the Cold War, the Gulf War, and the Iraq War.

A different brand of tax revolt is the tax protest. Tax protesters hold that the federal government has no authority to collect income taxes, and they cite various parts of the Constitution or offer other legal justifications to support their argument. The IRS denies many such claims on the web page "The Truth About Frivolous Tax Arguments."

signed by President George W. Bush, and the American Taxpayer Relief Act of 2012, signed by President Barack Obama.

IRS AUDITS

The IRS is most dreaded in its role as auditor of income tax filings. A tax audit is conducted to verify the accuracy of reported income, expenses, and credits. Less than 1 percent of tax returns are audited, according to IRS statistics.

If you're being audited by the IRS and your tax return was prepared by a professional firm, you should notify them and ask for advice on how to navigate the process.

Some audits are random; in other cases, the IRS computer system reports a possible inconsistency. The system compares your filing to those of taxpayers with similar financial circumstances. If your reported information is unusual compared to these norms, an IRS agent examines the return to assess whether it should be audited. The computer system also checks that figures on each tax return match information reported from other sources, such as tax forms submitted by employers. In addition, if you report business transactions with other individuals or organizations being audited, you may be audited as well.

Certain filers are more likely to trigger audits. High earners making over $200,000 a year are more likely to be audited than lower earners, according to The Balance. However, filers claiming no adjusted gross income also have a high likelihood of being audited. Filers who own their own small businesses or are self-employed are more likely to be audited. Their tax returns are more likely to be complicated, involving multiple forms. The IRS may audit these filers to check that they are not underreporting income or taking improper deductions. People who file paper returns are more likely to be audited as well because it's easier to make errors when calculating by hand rather than using software.

Filers who are selected for an audit are informed by mail—the IRS does not contact people by phone. The letter will likely request additional financial records to confirm income and deductions, or it will propose an adjustment to the amount of taxes owed. If the filer disagrees with the adjustment, he or she must provide documents as proof. According to Motley Fool, over 75 percent of audits are resolved through mail.

During an in-person audit, the filer meets with an agent to review tax information. Possible outcomes to either type of audit include no change, an agreement to IRS adjustments, or a disagreement with IRS findings. If the taxpayer disagrees, he or she can request a conference with an IRS manager or file an appeal.

The audit may find either that the filer overpaid or underpaid taxes. An overpayment results in a refund. An underpayment will most likely be considered negligence—a legitimate mistake. The taxpayer will pay the amount owed and sometimes an additional penalty. If the IRS suspects fraud or an attempt to evade taxes, however, the case may be referred to the IRS criminal investigation division. Evidence of fraud may include keeping two sets of business records or falsely claiming a dependent as a tax deduction.

The IRS is allowed three years after the filing date to initiate an audit. In cases of substantial errors, the IRS can investigate back six years. Filers should retain financial records at least that long as a precaution.

GETTING HELP

Whether you're a newbie or veteran to federal income taxes, you're likely to have questions as you prepare to file your return. The most authoritative source of information on income taxes is the IRS itself. The agency provides all tax forms along with instructions for each form, which are available on its website and through the mail. Filers can also find publications, recommendations, tax statistics, and changes in the tax code from year to year. The IRS site allows users to check the status of their tax account and find answers using an interactive tax assistant tool. Taxpayers earning under $66,000 can file taxes electronically for free using the IRS Free File software. Telephone assistance is also available, although call wait times

When choosing a tax professional such as a certified public accountant, ask about their credentials and whether they'd be available to represent you in case of an audit.

can be very long during tax season. The IRS offers tax assistance and services to people with disabilities as well.

Many people hire a tax professional such as a certified public accountant (CPA) to prepare their tax returns. The taxpayer provides the tax preparer with financial documents, and the preparer enters the information for the return. You might consider hiring a tax professional if your taxes are very complicated or if you want to be certain they're accurate. The advantages include saving time, guaranteeing accuracy, and possibly claiming deductions you might otherwise have missed. The disadvantages include the cost and the possibility that it might be difficult to schedule an appointment close to tax day.

Tax preparation software can provide many of the same advantages as professional tax services. The returns are likely to be accurate, and the software generally searches for relevant credits or deductions. Some packages offer a free basic option for simple returns and charge extra for additional services, such as filing self-employment income or accessing live customer support.

Certain free resources are also available for taxpayers who need help. People with moderate incomes and older Americans qualify for programs such as Volunteer Income Tax Assistance (VITA) and Tax Counseling for the Elderly (TCE). Some universities offer free legal clinics that provide services by students under supervision by qualified attorneys. Check your library or community center to see what programs are available in your area.

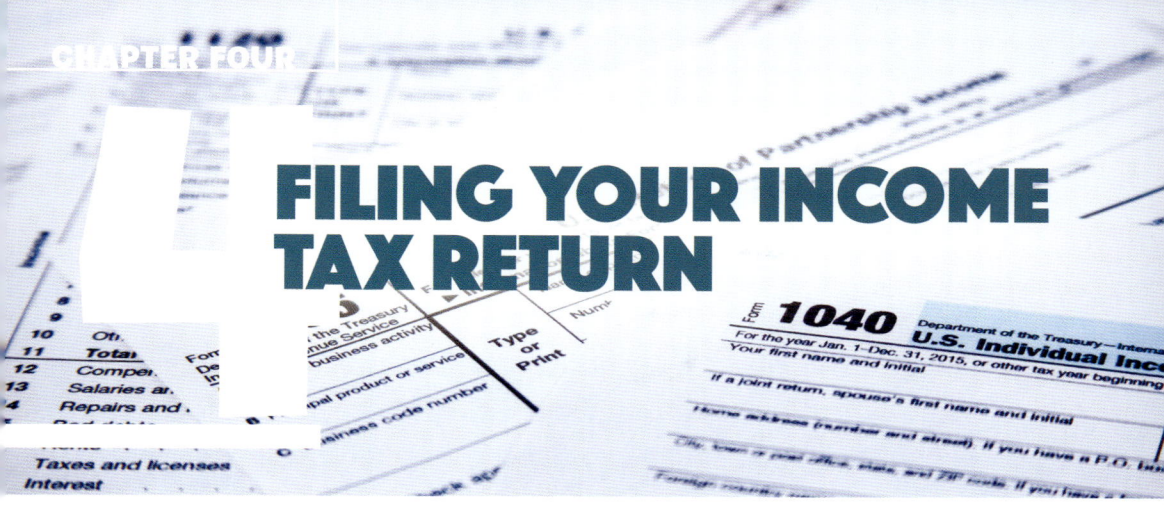

CHAPTER FOUR

FILING YOUR INCOME TAX RETURN

Before the existence of the internet, people would swarm post offices across the country on the income tax deadline date to mail their tax returns. Now, most Americans file their returns electronically—in 2018, the IRS anticipated that 90 percent of taxpayers would e-file. In general, taxpayers are required to file their tax returns by April 15 every year. There are a few exceptions—residents of Maine and Massachusetts have until April 17, for example, and American citizens living abroad are granted an extension until June 15.

People line up inside a Manhattan post office in New York City on April 15 in order to mail off their tax returns before the midnight tax deadline.

If a taxpayer is unable to complete a return by the deadline, he or she can file a form for a six-month extension, until October 15. In most cases, the extension is granted automatically. The request form must be filed by April 15. An extension for filing a tax return, however, does not change the deadline for paying taxes. If the filer owes taxes, the unpaid balance may be subject to penalties. The penalty for not filing a tax return or extension request is more severe than the penalty for late payments.

PAYING AS YOU GO

Most workers have taxes deducted automatically from their paychecks and paid to the government throughout the year. There are advantages and disadvantages to this system. If taxes weren't withheld, taxpayers would be responsible for paying the entire amount when filing tax returns, which could create a financial burden. On the other hand, some people would prefer to receive the money and manage it themselves until tax day.

Tax withholding is set up by the employer. A new employee fills out an IRS Form W-4, entering information such as marital status and number of dependents. (A dependent is a child or other relative who depends on the earner for more than half of their financial support.) This information, known as your allowances, is used to estimate the amount of taxes the employee will owe annually and determine the amount deducted from each paycheck.

The amount withheld is an estimate of what an employee owes in taxes. Employees can adjust the allowances on their W-4 forms to have more or less money deducted from each paycheck. The IRS charges an underpayment penalty if the final amount of tax owed is significantly more than the amount withheld. If you want to confirm that the appropriate amount of taxes are being withheld from your paycheck, you can use the online IRS Withholding Calculator to check whether you should update your W-4 information.

When you file your tax return, you may determine that you've overpaid or underpaid throughout the year through withholding. If you've overpaid, you receive a refund. If you've underpaid, you have to pay additional taxes.

People who are self-employed do not submit W-4 forms. Instead, they estimate the amount of taxes they will owe and make quarterly payments throughout the year.

YOUR TAX BRACKET

The first step in filing taxes is establishing whether or not you need to complete a return. Single filers

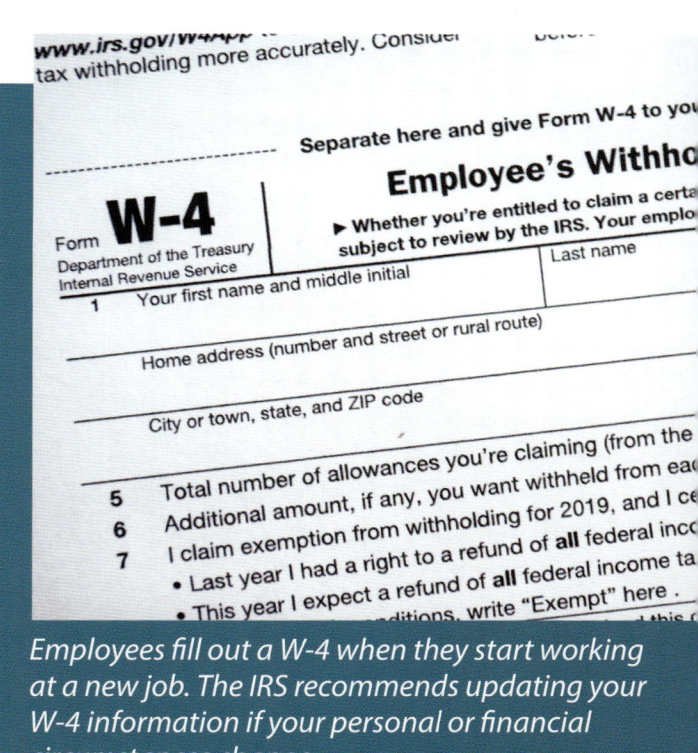

Employees fill out a W-4 when they start working at a new job. The IRS recommends updating your W-4 information if your personal or financial circumstances change.

Before you begin filling out tax forms, you should determine whether you need to file taxes, assemble all relevant tax forms, and check for recent changes to tax laws.

under the age of sixty-five who earn less than $12,000 in gross income generally do not need to file a tax return, for example. (This category includes filers who are claimed as dependents.) The income threshold depends on filing status. If you qualify as a head of household—meaning that you're unmarried and support a child or other relative—the income threshold is higher.

There are certain other situations in which taxpayers must file a return even if their income falls below the threshold. People who are self-employed must file a return if they report over $400 in earnings. If you're owed a refund, you must file a return to receive it. The IRS Interactive Tax Assistant can help taxpayers determine whether they need to file a return.

Filing status is also one of the factors that determine an individual's tax rate. Tax brackets are the percentages of taxes paid on income. There are seven tax brackets used to calculate how much a taxpayer will owe: 10 percent, 12 percent, 22 percent, 24 percent, 32 percent, 35 percent, and 37 percent. Your filing status determines the dollar range of each bracket. For example, for a taxpayer whose filing status is single, the 10 percent bracket is $0 to $9,525; the 12 percent bracket is $9,526 to $38,700; the 22 percent bracket is $38,701 to $82,500, the 24 percent bracket is $82,501 to $157,500; the 32 percent bracket is $157,501 to $200,000; the 35 percent bracket is $200,001 to $500,000; and the 37 percent bracket is over $500,001.

The tax brackets determine the amount of tax paid on different portions of a taxpayer's income. Someone whose earnings fall within a certain percent bracket doesn't pay that rate on his or her total income. A single taxpayer earning $40,000, for example, would pay 10 percent on the first $9,525 of income (which works out to $952.50), 12 percent on earnings from $9,526 to $38,700 (which works out to $3,501), and 22 percent on income above $38,700 (which works out to $286). The total taxes owed add up to $4,739.50, which is much less than if the entire income had been taxed at the bracket of 22 percent (that amount would be $8,800). Don't worry about the math when you're doing your taxes—percentages are calculated automatically or listed on tables.

There are separate sets of brackets for filing statuses that include single filers; married, filing jointly; married, filing separately; and head of household. There is no separate set of brackets for earners who qualify as dependents.

FIGURING OUT THE FORMS

As you complete your tax return, make sure that you have the relevant instruction books for each form, which are available through the IRS website and on paper. Many publications begin by describing what's new for the tax year. There are always annual updates, and the Tax Cuts and Jobs Act produced some of the biggest changes to the forms and processes seen in years. If you consult additional resources, double-check that they are up to date for the most recent tax year.

Before you begin entering information, assemble all of the key forms for reporting income. You must pay income taxes on any income you received from a job, including wages, salaries, tips, commissions, and business income. You must also pay taxes on income from investment interest and various other sources, such as rental income, alimony, winnings from gambling, and unemployment compensation.

You'll have received tax forms from many of your sources of income stating how much you were paid during the course of the tax year. W-2 forms, sent by employers, describe earnings and how much tax was withheld. The 1099-MISC forms describe miscellaneous earnings from which taxes were not withheld, such as self-employment income. The 1099-INT forms report earnings such as interest or dividends from savings accounts or investments. The 1098 forms describe interest paid on student loans or mortgages. These are just a few of the most common tax documents describing income or expenses.

Almost all taxpayers fill out an IRS 1040 form, which is the basic form used to file a tax return. You fill in basic taxpayer information, such as your name, address, Social Security number, filing status, and whether you qualify as a dependent. You then add up your sources of income, enter deductions and credits, and calculate taxes owed.

Many of the entries may require filling out and attaching additional forms. Some of these forms are identified as schedules. Schedule 2, for example, applies to people who owe alternative minimum tax (AMT)—a tax on

Preparing your tax return requires calculating your taxes, credits, and deductions. You may determine that you owe taxes, or you may receive a refund.

higher earners intended to prevent the wealthy from using tax breaks to avoid paying taxes. Schedule 4 tallies up other taxes, such as self-employment tax, that are added to regular income tax.

There are also several schedules identified by letter that are commonly used by taxpayers. Schedule B reports taxable interest and dividends over $1,500. Schedule C reports a business profit or loss. Schedule D reports capital gains and losses, such as through selling or trading stocks, bonds, or real estate.

Hundreds of other forms exist that pertain to specific tax situations as well. Filers who e-file their tax returns generally

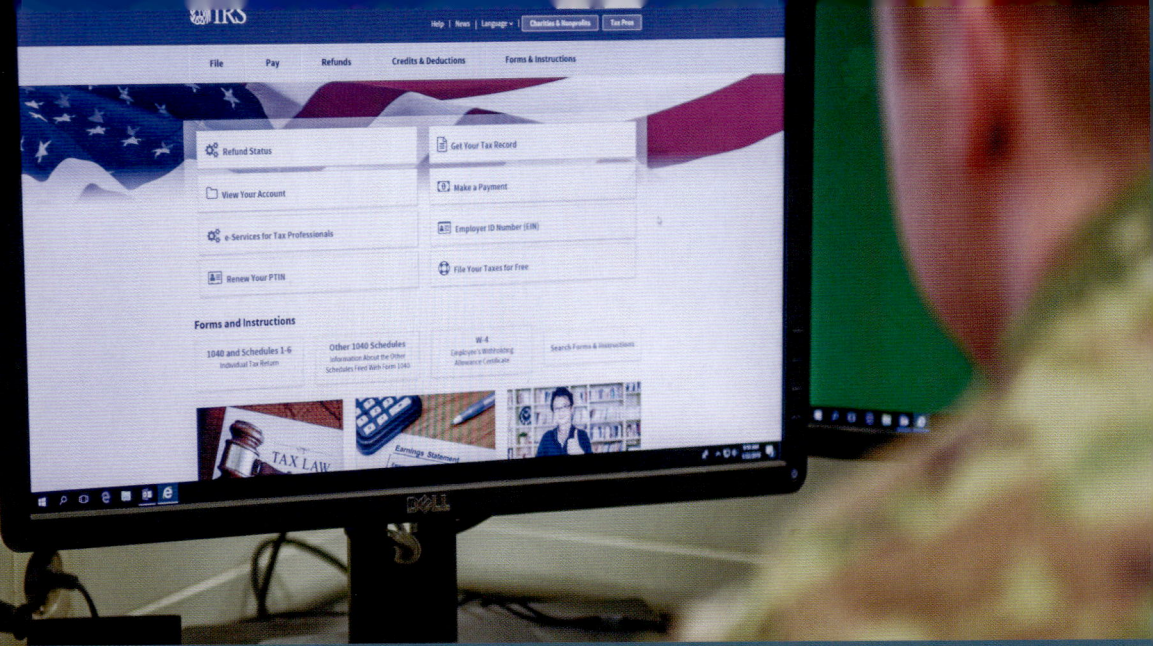

A US Army soldier stationed in Germany accesses tax information through the IRS website. Military personnel serving abroad may qualify for automatic tax extensions.

do not have to worry about assembling a set of forms, as it's done for them by software.

KEEPING TRACK OF DEDUCTIONS AND CREDITS

Many of the forms that make up a tax return pertain to deductions and credits. These can reduce the amount of taxes you owe. When you claim a deduction or credit, make sure you keep the relevant documents proving that your reporting is accurate. These may include receipts, records of mileage driven for business, or financial statements.

CAPITAL GAINS TAX

Capital gains are profits made on investments such as property or shares of stock. When the investment increases in value, the investor makes a capital gain. If the value decreases, the result is a capital loss. An investor's capital gains may be offset by capital losses. The investor does not have to pay capital gains taxes until selling the investment and making a profit. Therefore, investors may time their sales to minimize the amount of capital gains taxes.

Tax rates for capital gains depend on the circumstances. Short-term capital gains, held for less than twelve months, are taxed at the same rate as ordinary income. Long-term capital gains, held for over twelve months, are taxed at lower rates. There are exceptions depending on the situation and the particular type of asset. Art and real estate, for example, are subject to a different set of rules and rates.

For investors who make capital gains for a living, such as day traders or real estate developers, their profits are taxed as business income rather than capital gains. Homeowners who are selling their primary residence are exempt for up to $250,000 of capital gains, according to Motley Fool.

Deductions are adjustments to income. They are subtracted from taxable income, which means that you don't have to pay taxes on the amount that is deducted. Schedule A reports a number of itemized deductions that filers commonly claim, including medical and dental expenses, state and local taxes, mortgage interest, charitable contributions, and casualty and theft losses. Schedule 1 also lists various deductions, such as educator expenses and student loan interest deduction, as well as different forms of additional income.

When you claim a deduction, read the requirements carefully. Limits apply to many deductions. The floor for claiming qualifying medical expenses in 2019, for example, is 10 percent of adjusted gross income (AGI), meaning that medical expenses must exceed 10 percent of your AGI—prohibitively high for many filers. If a person earning $100,000 annually had $15,000 in eligible medical expenses, only $5,000 would qualify for the deduction. Ceilings apply to

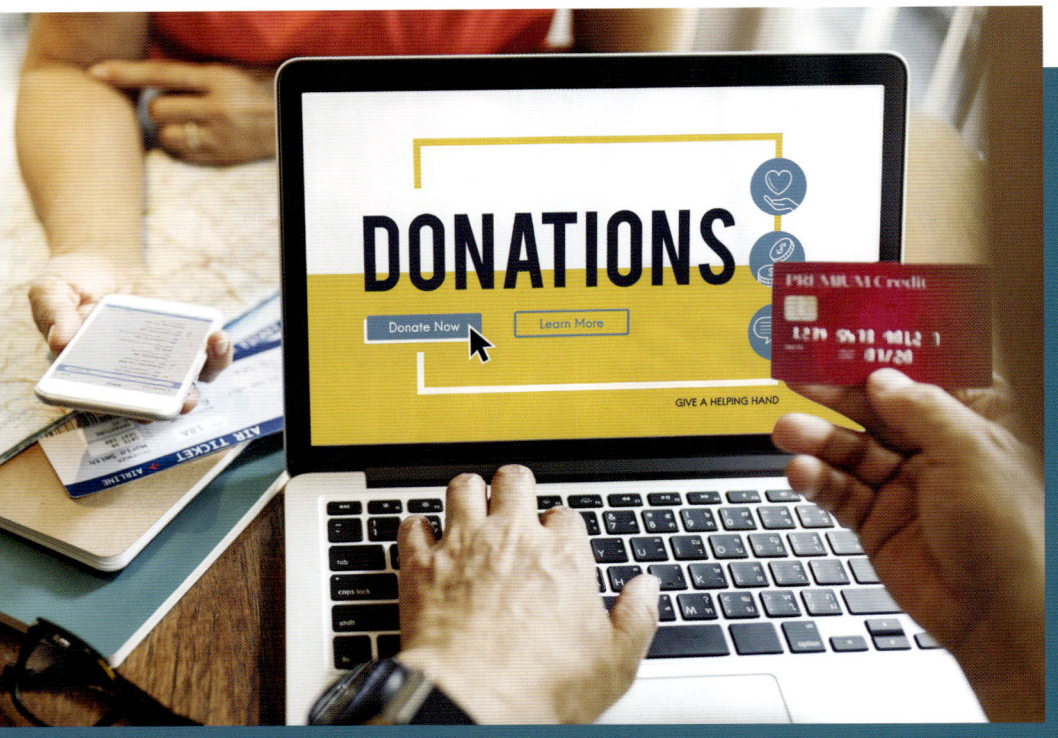

Some charitable donations are tax deductible, but you should double-check that the donation qualifies and fill out the relevant tax forms to claim the deduction.

some deductions as well. The deduction for making certain types of charitable contributions cannot exceed 60 percent of AGI, for example. If a person earning $100,000 annually donated $75,000 in eligible charitable contributions, only $60,000 of it could be claimed as a deduction in a year.

Tax returns give filers an option of taking a standard deduction or listing itemized deductions in Schedule A. A standard deduction is a set amount deducted from taxable income. For 2019, it was set at $12,200 for a filer with a tax status of single. Most filers choose to take the standard deduction rather than itemizing deductions. Generally, listing itemized deductions is worthwhile only if the total amount exceeds the standard deduction.

People who file Schedule C can also deduct certain expenses from their business profits. Examples include office expenses, utilities, travel, maintenance, and business use of one's home or vehicle.

Tax credits reduce tax payments. A tax credit is subtracted from the amount of taxes owed. A tax credit called the Earned Income Credit (EIC) reduces the tax burden on certain low-income taxpayers. Credits such as the American Opportunity Credit aim to make education more affordable for low- and middle-income families by issuing a credit for tuition and other qualifying expenses. The Child Tax Credit grants a credit per child to taxpayers earning under a certain income threshold. Making contributions to retirement accounts can result in credits for some taxpayers. Other credits are granted for covering adoption costs and making certain energy-efficient purchases, such as solar water heaters.

10 GREAT QUESTIONS

TO ASK A CERTIFIED PUBLIC ACCOUNTANT

1   What forms and other financial documents do I have to assemble for my income tax preparer?

2   Am I required to file an income tax return?

3   Are there any changes to the tax code this year that affect me?

4   If I have self-employment income and investment income as well as my regular income, how do these affect my tax return?

5   Am I eligible for any educational tax credits if I'm a student with expenses related to education?

6   Are there any income tax regulations or deductions that affect my field of work?

7   Are there any strategies I can use to benefit more from deductions or credits on my income tax return?

8   Will I get a refund or owe income taxes?

9   What are the sales tax rates imposed in my city and state?

10   How are property taxes calculated in my city?

CHAPTER FIVE

STATE AND LOCAL TAXES

Every state government has its own tax system that raises revenue from a variety of sources. They rely on different combinations of tax sources, write their own tax laws, and set rates to meet revenue needs. Some of their specific taxes might seem quirky to outsiders. Maine taxes wild blueberries, its state fruit and one of its leading crops. Hawaii, which values its natural heritage, offers a $3,000 state tax deduction to people who own particularly remarkable trees. Maryland charges a sewer and septic fee to

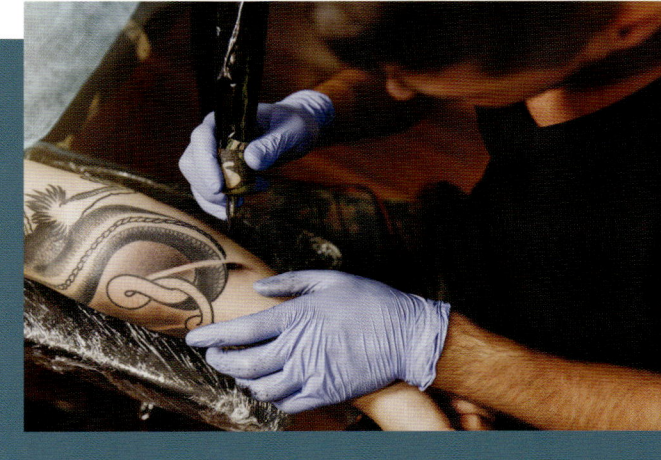

Anyone getting a tattoo in Arkansas should be prepared to pay a 6 percent tax on the service. Body piercings are subject to the tax as well.

help conserve the Chesapeake Bay. Colorado taxes nonessential packaging, meaning that a coffee cup lid is taxed, but not the cup itself. Arkansas imposes a 6 percent tax on getting a tattoo, and New York charges a tax on bagels that are sliced—but not on uncut bagels.

TAXING ON MANY LEVELS

Many taxes that are collected on a federal level are also imposed by states and even local governments. Rates are generally lower at the state and local level than federal, and they can vary widely from one state to another.

Most states collect a state income tax. Eight do not as of 2021: Alaska, Florida, Nevada, South Dakota, Tennessee, Texas, Washington, and Wyoming. Many e-file tax return programs prepare state tax returns as well as federal, sometimes at no additional cost. State income tax returns are due on the same day as federal income tax returns in most states, but a few set a later filing deadline in late April or early May. In many states, filing for an extension on your federal income tax return automatically grants a taxpayer a six-month extension on state income tax returns as well. Specific laws vary, so check the requirements in your state.

Overall, state income taxes were the second-largest source of state revenue (behind sales taxes), bringing in $398 billion according to the US Census Bureau 2017 Annual Survey of State Tax Collections. California took in the most revenue, at $155 billion, and it also had the highest tax rate of 13.3 percent in 2018, although the state charges a progressive tax rate and only filers earning over $1 million pay that rate, according to The Balance. Most states have a progressive system, with a wide variety of ranges between the lowest and highest rates, as

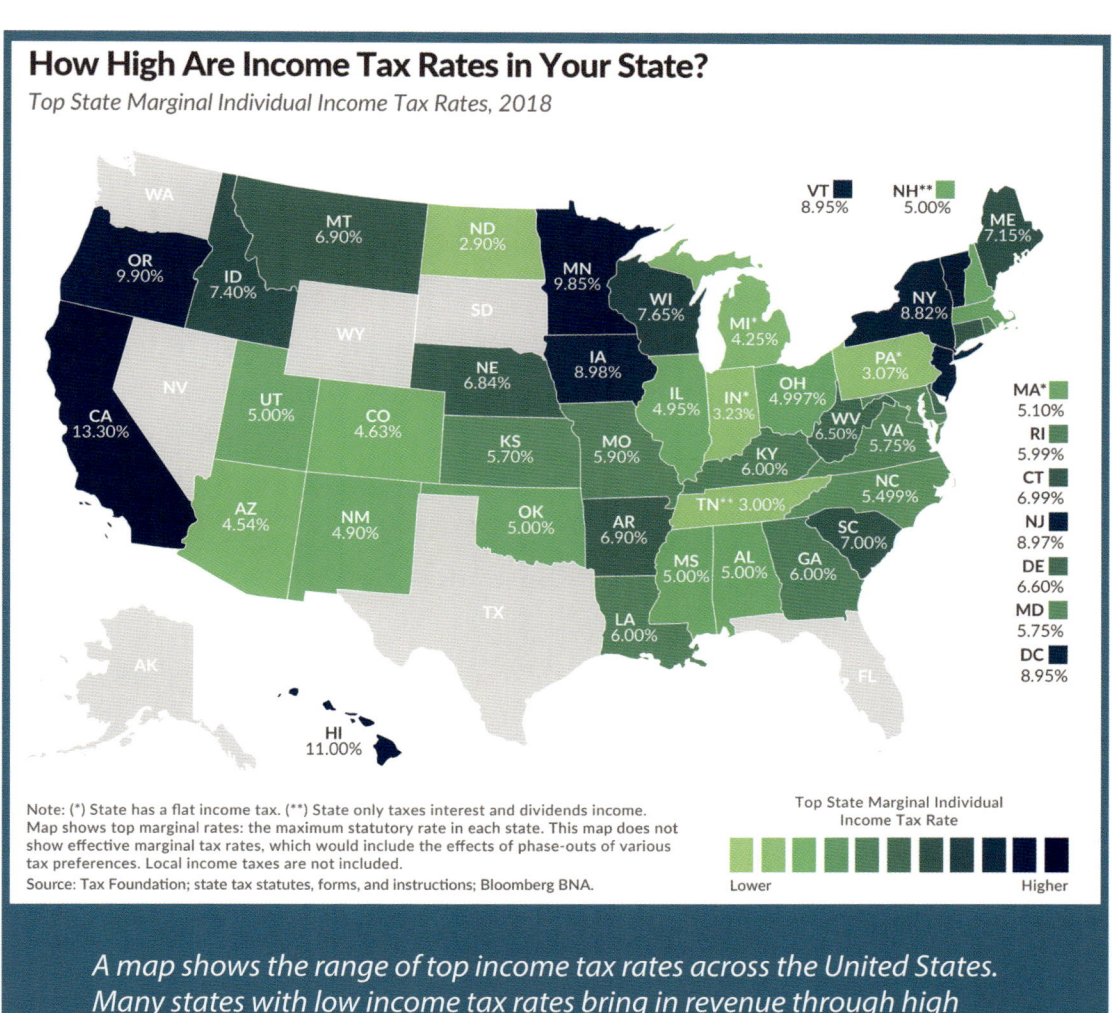

How High Are Income Tax Rates in Your State?
Top State Marginal Individual Income Tax Rates, 2018

VT 8.95%
NH** 5.00%
ME 7.15%
WA
MT 6.90%
ND 2.90%
OR 9.90%
ID 7.40%
MN 9.85%
WI 7.65%
NY 8.82%
SD
MI* 4.25%
PA* 3.07%
NV
NE 6.84%
IA 8.98%
IL 4.95%
IN* 3.23%
OH 4.997%
UT 5.00%
CO 4.63%
WV 6.50%
VA 5.75%
CA 13.30%
KS 5.70%
MO 5.90%
KY 6.00%
NC 5.499%
AZ 4.54%
NM 4.90%
OK 5.00%
AR 6.90%
TN** 3.00%
SC 7.00%
MS 5.00%
AL 5.00%
GA 6.00%
TX
LA 6.00%
AK
FL
HI 11.00%

MA* 5.10%
RI 5.99%
CT 6.99%
NJ 8.97%
DE 6.60%
MD 5.75%
DC 8.95%

Note: (*) State has a flat income tax. (**) State only taxes interest and dividends income. Map shows top marginal rates: the maximum statutory rate in each state. This map does not show effective marginal tax rates, which would include the effects of phase-outs of various tax preferences. Local income taxes are not included.
Source: Tax Foundation; state tax statutes, forms, and instructions; Bloomberg BNA.

Top State Marginal Individual Income Tax Rate
Lower   Higher

A map shows the range of top income tax rates across the United States. Many states with low income tax rates bring in revenue through high property or sales taxes.

well as the cap for the highest tax bracket. Eight states impose a flat tax, ranging between 3 and 6 percent. States may also allow for deductions to income and credits to tax payments.

In four states, local governments can charge income taxes. In nine, local governments have some form of withholding or payroll tax on earners who work in the district. Tax systems include flat rates, progressive rates, or a fixed dollar amount for every worker.

Every state collects excise taxes on certain specific goods and activities, although excise taxes are not a major source of revenue in most states. All states have a motor fuel tax that is used to fund road and highway projects. Like the federal government, states also impose "sin taxes" on products such as alcohol and tobacco, as well as winnings from gambling. Some states impose a hotel tax or an amusement tax, such as on tickets for sports events, concerts, and other forms of entertainment. Municipalities and counties can also levy excise taxes.

Two excise taxes new in the 2000s are the soda tax and marijuana tax. A few cities have enacted a tax on soda and other sugary drinks on the grounds that soda is a major contributor to the obesity epidemic. Supporters claim that the tax will cause residents to reconsider buying sugary drinks and that the revenue it generates can support worthy programs. Recreational marijuana also has the potential to generate significant tax revenue in states where it's legal. Since Colorado became the first state to allow the sale of recreational marijuana in 2014, sales exceeded $6 billion, according to CNBC in 2019, generating $927 million in tax revenue. Many states have followed Colorado's lead in legalizing marijuana and imposing high taxes.

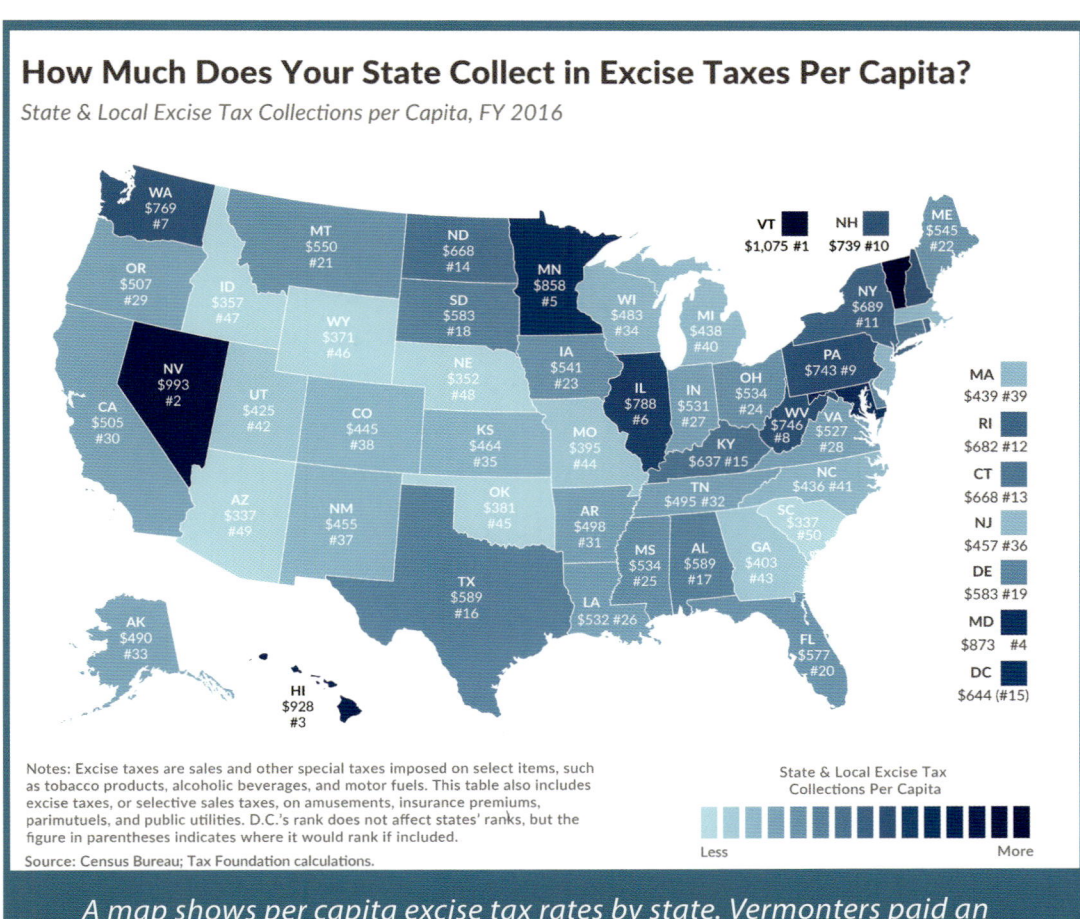

How Much Does Your State Collect in Excise Taxes Per Capita?

State & Local Excise Tax Collections per Capita, FY 2016

Notes: Excise taxes are sales and other special taxes imposed on select items, such as tobacco products, alcoholic beverages, and motor fuels. This table also includes excise taxes, or selective sales taxes, on amusements, insurance premiums, parimutuels, and public utilities. D.C.'s rank does not affect states' ranks, but the figure in parentheses indicates where it would rank if included.

Source: Census Bureau; Tax Foundation calculations.

State & Local Excise Tax Collections Per Capita

Less — More

A map shows per capita excise tax rates by state. Vermonters paid an average of $1,075 in excise taxes in 2016, while South Carolinians paid only $337.

Many states impose estate taxes. The tax rates are lower than federal estate taxes, but the tax threshold is also lower in some states. A few states impose an inheritance tax on heirs. The highest rate falls between 10 and 20 percent for both estate and inheritance taxes, according to NerdWallet. The rate for an inheritance tax generally depends on how closely the heir is related to the deceased, however. A spouse is exempted from inheritance taxes, and children are taxed at a lower rate than more distant relatives.

SALES AND USE TAXES

Sales tax is a consumption tax on goods and services. A percentage is added to a customer's total sale when he or she is ready to pay. The retailer submits the tax to the government.

Sales tax is paid only by the end user, who makes a purchase from a retailer. Producers who buy goods to resell—including when they're component parts of something they sell—do not have to pay sales tax. A manufacturing company does not have to pay sales tax on materials used in constructing its products, for example, and a retail company does not have to pay sales tax on goods that it will resell in a store. These purchasers can obtain a resale certificate that exempts them from sales tax at checkout. Procedures for using a resale certificate vary from one state to another. The purchaser must charge sales tax when selling the item to the end user, however, unless it is sold to another producer intending to resell.

Some items are exempt from sales tax or are taxed at a lower rate in many states. Examples include food, medicine, and clothing. In some states, a sales tax exemption may be capped at a certain level. Only the first $175 of a single article of clothing might be tax exempt, for instance. Certain nonprofit groups such as charitable, religious, and educational organizations may be exempt from paying or collecting sales tax as well, depending on state law.

Maine's 5.5 percent sales tax rate is shown on a receipt. Some places also impose local sales taxes that significantly increase the overall rate.

VALUE-ADDED TAX

The value-added tax (VAT) is one of the most common types of tax in the world, but it's not collected in the United States. In many countries, a VAT functions as a national consumption tax. Unlike a sales tax, which is added onto the final price paid by the buyer, a VAT is collected at different points during the process of manufacturing a product. The basic concept is that value is added at every step of production, and the VAT is imposed on each level that value increases. For example, raw materials may be sold to a company that refines them; the resultant components may be sold to a manufacturer that builds a product; the manufacturer sells the product to a retailer, who sells it to a consumer. At every step, a percentage of the profit is paid as a VAT.

Implementing a VAT in the United States at a national level would require significant legislation, and introducing a vast new tax would not be popular with voters. Nonetheless, some economists point out that a VAT would collect from a broad tax base, raise substantial revenue efficiently, and close tax loopholes. Critics claim that a complex administrative system would be required to track every VAT at every level, that the states would object to the federal government imposing its own consumption tax, and that a VAT is strongly regressive—it would impose a greater burden on the poor than on the rich.

In many states, sales tax is a significant source of revenue. According to the US Census Bureau 2017 Annual Survey of State Tax Collections, sales tax brought in the largest total, at about $453 billion. Rates vary widely—California has the highest state-level sales tax rate, at 7.25 percent, with Indiana, Mississippi, Rhode Island, and Tennessee close behind at

7 percent, according to the Tax Foundation. A few states impose no sales tax.

States with a moderate state sales tax rate can still rank as having high overall sales tax rates when local sales taxes are included. Local sales taxes tend to range from 0 to over 5 percent. Some states, such as Tennessee, Louisiana, and Arkansas, have average sales tax rates of over 9.4 percent when local sales taxes are included. New York, Colorado, and Oklahoma also have high average local sales taxes, between 4 and 5 percent.

High local sales taxes can affect consumers and businesses in an area. Customers may cross city or county lines to make purchases at a lower sales tax rate. Businesses may choose a location just outside the border of a city or county to avoid collecting higher sales tax rates.

Many states also collect use taxes, which are similar to sales taxes. Use taxes are levied on goods bought out of state or on property that is leased or rented—cases in which sales tax was not paid. People who buy goods online from a company outside their state, for example, may be subject to use taxes. Unlike sales tax, use taxes are generally reported and paid by the customer, not the seller.

PROPERTY TAXES

Property tax—the term is generally interchangeable with "real estate tax"—is a tax paid by owners on land and items such as buildings that are permanently attached to the land. Some states, however, also tax "personal property," such as cars, equipment, and certain personal possessions. Businesses as well as individuals are required to pay property taxes.

Property taxes are a relatively minor source of state revenue. According to the Tax Policy Center, only thirty-six states collected property taxes in 2016, bringing in a total revenue of $16 billion. Property taxes are a significant source of local revenue, however. Local governments collected $487 billion from property taxes in 2016. The revenue funds local services, such as schools, policing, infrastructure, and water and sanitation services.

Laws, rates, criteria, and procedures regarding property taxes vary widely across the country and even from one local jurisdiction to another. In some states and

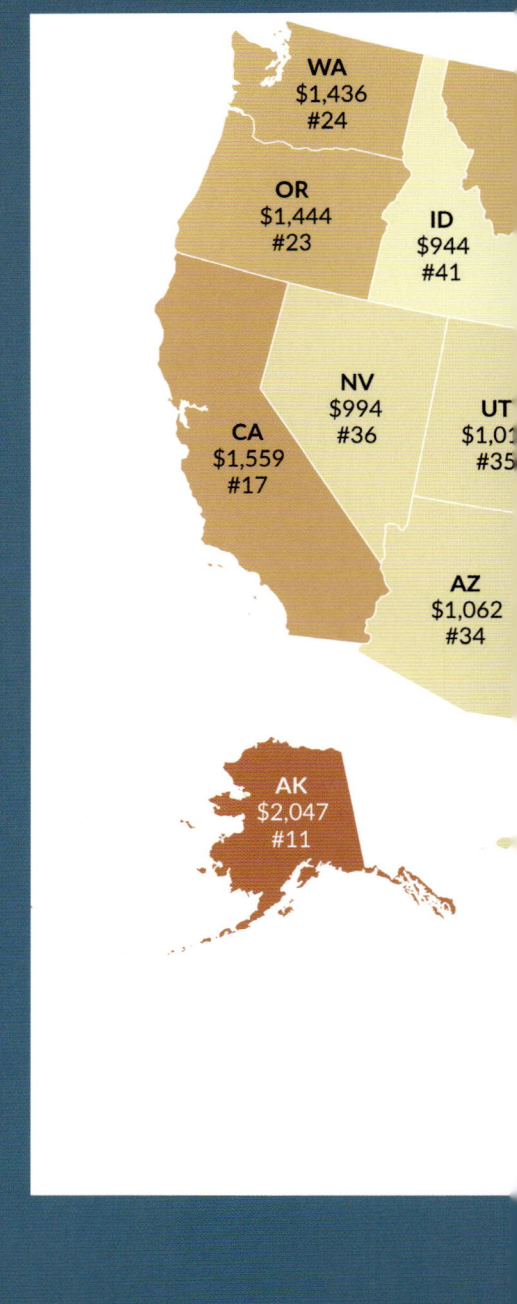

HOW MUCH DOES YOUR STATE COLLECT IN PROPERTY TAXES PER CAPITA?

State & Local Property Tax Collections per Capita, FY 2016

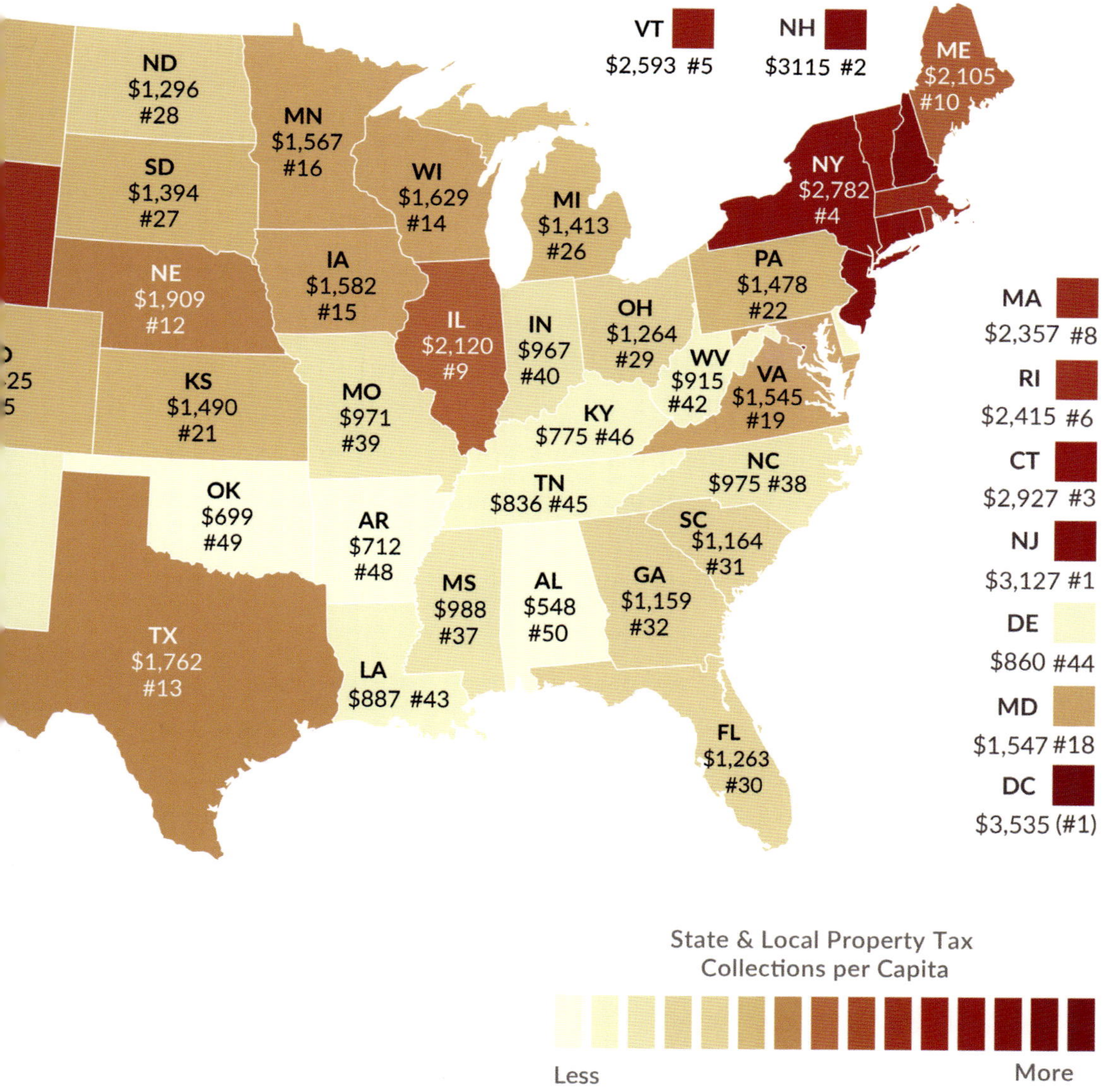

VT $2,593 #5

NH $3115 #2

ME $2,105 #10

ND $1,296 #28

MN $1,567 #16

SD $1,394 #27

WI $1,629 #14

MI $1,413 #26

NY $2,782 #4

PA $1,478 #22

NE $1,909 #12

IA $1,582 #15

IL $2,120 #9

IN $967 #40

OH $1,264 #29

WV $915 #42

VA $1,545 #19

KS $1,490 #21

MO $971 #39

KY $775 #46

NC $975 #38

OK $699 #49

AR $712 #48

TN $836 #45

SC $1,164 #31

TX $1,762 #13

LA $887 #43

MS $988 #37

AL $548 #50

GA $1,159 #32

FL $1,263 #30

25 5

MA $2,357 #8

RI $2,415 #6

CT $2,927 #3

NJ $3,127 #1

DE $860 #44

MD $1,547 #18

DC $3,535 (#1)

State & Local Property Tax Collections per Capita

Less   More

A map shows the range of per capita property taxes by state. The highest property tax collections occurred in Washington, DC, at $3,535 per resident.

cities, high property taxes can represent a significant financial burden on residents. These places may offer great schools and public services, but a high tax bill can discourage potential homebuyers from looking in the area.

Property tax is an example of an ad valorem tax (from Latin, meaning, "according to value"), which is based on the assessed value of the property. Property is officially appraised by an assessor who sets a taxable value—the process varies from one locality to another. Sometimes the assessed rate is the same as the market value, which is the price the property would sell for. Other times the assessed rate is lower. There are generally procedures that allow an owner to contest the assessed value of property. The tax bill is the property value multiplied by the tax rate, which must be paid according to the schedule set by local authorities.

Property owners may be eligible for various exemptions, deductions, limits, and credits that reduce their property taxes. Many jurisdictions grant a homestead exemption or deduction for owners who reside on the property. Senior citizens, people with disabilities, and veterans may be eligible for tax breaks or assistance programs. Nonprofit groups and churches are generally exempt from paying property taxes, and some land use, such as agriculture, may be taxed at a different rate. Local administrators sometimes offer property tax breaks to lure new businesses.

Property tax credit and exemption programs vary widely from one state to another. In New York, for example, taxpayers can apply for a rebate from the state on property taxes paid to fund local school districts through its State School Tax Relief (STAR) Program. Any property owner should research property tax relief measures offered by the state or local government.

Paying taxes is a civic duty required of all Americans—it enables the government to provide essential services. As you reach adulthood and engage in more financial transactions—such as making investments, buying property, and earning more money—you'll be obligated to pay more taxes. Certain other life milestones, such as paying for your education, starting a family, and planning for retirement, will also have implications for your tax situation. It's important that you understand your rights and responsibilities as a taxpayer to help ensure your financial security.

GLOSSARY

consumption tax A tax paid on buying a good or service, such as sales or excise taxes.

deficit A shortfall resulting from the government spending more money than it takes in as revenue.

dependent A child or other qualifying relative who relies on the taxpayer for financial support.

employee A person who works for an employer for wages or salary.

estate tax A tax levied on an individual's estate after his or her death.

excise tax A tax on a specific good or service. An indirect tax, the excise tax is usually collected from the producer or retailer, which passes it onto the consumer by increasing the sales price.

fiscal Relating to money and finances, especially government revenues such as taxes.

income taxes Taxes on money that someone has earned, as well as unearned income such as interest, paid by both businesses and individuals.

interest A charge paid on money that has been borrowed.

payroll taxes Deductions from an employee's pay that funds Social Security and Medicare programs.

progressive tax A tax that takes a larger proportion from high-income earners than from low-income earners.

property taxes Taxes on real estate and sometimes other types of personal property.

proportional tax A tax that takes the same proportion from all earners.

refund Money returned by the government to taxpayers who have paid more tax than they owe.

regressive tax A tax that takes a larger proportion from low-income earners than from high-income earners.

revenue The income that a nation takes in from taxes.

salary The pay that an employee receives from an employer, typically paid for a regular work period, such as weekly or monthly.

tariff A tax on goods imported from other countries.

tax A required payment to the government, usually assessed as a percentage of the value of the income, property, cost, etc. being taxed.

tax credit An amount of money that can be deducted from taxes owed.

tax deduction An amount of money that can be deducted from the value of something (such as income or property) subject to taxation.

value-added tax (VAT) A kind of consumption or sales tax that is considered an indirect tax. VAT is levied on each step of the production or distribution of a product or service (from the raw materials to manufacture to final retail price), based on the value added at each step, and is included in the cost to the final consumer.

wages The pay that an employee receives from an employer, typically paid at an hourly rate.

Board of Governors of the Federal Reserve System

20th Street and Constitution Avenue NW

Washington, DC 20551

(202) 452-3000

Website: https://www.federalreserve.gov

Facebook and Twitter: @federalreserve

The Federal Reserve is the central bank of the United States, charged with promoting maximum employment, price stability, and moderate long-term interest rates. Federal Reserve economists also conduct research and analysis on a wide range of economic areas.

Canada Revenue Agency

555 MacKenzie Avenue

Ottawa, ON K1A 0L5

Canada

(613) 941-3121

Website: https://www.canada.ca/en/revenue-agency.html

Facebook and Twitter: @CanRevAgency

The Canada Revenue Agency administers Canadian tax legislation as well as programs related to the tax system.

Internal Revenue Service (IRS)

1111 Constitution Avenue NW

Washington, DC 20224

(202) 622-5000

Website: https://www.irs.gov

Facebook: @IRS

Twitter and Instagram: @IRSnews

The IRS is the bureau charged with collecting taxes and
enforcing internal revenue laws in the United States.

Official Guide to Government and Services

(844) 872-4681

Website: https://www.usa.gov

Facebook, Twitter, and Instagram: @USAGov

The official website of the United States provides
information on government programs, departments and
agencies, and their services. It also offers information
about money and taxes, small business, laws, voting,
jobs and careers, disasters and emergencies, and
consumer safety, among other issues.

Social Security Administration (SSA)

Office of Public Inquiries

1100 West High Rise

6401 Security Boulevard

Baltimore, MD 21235

(800) 772-1213

Website: https://www.ssa.gov

Facebook and Twitter: @socialsecurity

The Social Security Administration provides benefits to
retirees, survivors, and people with disabilities.

Treasury Board of Canada
90 Elgin Street, 8th Floor
Ottawa, ON K1A 0R5
Canada
(877) 636-0656
Website: https://www.canada.ca/en/treasury-board-
   secretariat.html
Twitter: @TBS_Canada
The Treasury Board oversees government spending
   in Canada.

US Department of the Treasury
1500 Pennsylvania Avenue NW
Washington, DC 20220
(202) 622-2000
Website: https://home.treasury.gov
Facebook and Twitter: @USTreasury
Instagram: @treasurydept
The US Department of the Treasury administers federal
   finances by collecting taxes, managing the public debt,
   paying bills, and issuing currency.

FOR FURTHER READING

Anderson, Max. *Where the Money Lies: A Non-Partisan Guide to Trump Economics*. Indianapolis, IN: Dog Ear Publishing, 2018.

Bissinger, Caleb. *Taxes and Society's Priorities*. New York, NY: Greenhaven Publishing, 2018.

Boneparth, Douglas A., and Heather J. Boneparth. *The Millennial Money Fix: What You Need to Know About Budgeting, Debt, and Finding Financial Freedom*. Wayne, NJ: Career Press, 2017.

Burman, Leonard, and Joel Slemrod. *Taxes in America*. 2nd ed. New York, NY: Oxford University Press, 2019.

Davidson, Liz. *What Your Financial Advisor Isn't Telling You: The 10 Essential Truths You Need to Know About Your Money*. Boston, MA: Mariner Books, 2017.

Doyle, Nancy. *Manage Your Financial Life: Just Starting Out*. Glencoe, IL: The Doyle Group, 2018.

Duignan, Brian, and Carolyn DeCarlo, eds. *The U.S. Constitution and the Separation of Powers*. New York, NY: Britannica Educational Publishing, 2019.

Garman, Thomas E., and Raymond E. Forgue. *Personal Finance*. 13th ed. Boston, MA: Cengage Learning, 2017.

Idzikowski, Lisa, ed. *The Federal Budget and Government Spending*. New York, NY: Greenhaven Publishing, 2019.

McGuire, Kara. *Cover Your Assets: The Teens' Guide to Protecting Their Money and Their Stuff*. North Mankato, MN: Compass Point Books, 2015.

McGuire, Kara. *Smart Spending: The Teens' Guide to Cash, Credit, and Life's Costs*. North Mankato, MN: Compass Point Books, 2015.

Tyson, Eric. *Personal Finance in Your 20s*. Hoboken, NJ: John Wiley & Sons, 2016.

Weeks, Marcus, and Derek Braddon. *Heads Up Money*. New York, NY: DK Publishing, 2017.

BIBLIOGRAPHY

Amadeo, Kimberly. "US Corporate Income Tax Rate, Its History and the Effective Rate." The Balance, January 16, 2019. https://www.thebalance.com/corporate-income-tax-definition-history-effective-rate-3306024.

Backman, Maurie. "5 Things to Know About Tax Audits." Motley Fool, March 6, 2019. https://www.fool.com/retirement/2019/03/06/5-things-to-know-about-tax-audits.aspx.

Bell, Kay. "Estate Tax: How It Works and Which States Have One." NerdWallet, October 12, 2018. https://www.nerdwallet.com/blog/taxes/which-states-have-estate-inheritance-taxes.

Bellafiore, Robert. "Summary of the Latest Federal Income Tax Data, 2018 Update." Tax Foundation, November 13, 2018. https://taxfoundation.org/summary-latest-federal-income-tax-data-2018-update.

Bieber, Christy. "How to File Your Taxes: A Beginner's Guide." Motley Fool, February 20, 2019. https://www.fool.com/taxes/2019/02/20/how-to-file-your-taxes-a-beginners-guide.aspx.

Bird, Beverly. "The History of the U.S. Federal Tax System." The Balance, January 28, 2019. https://www.thebalance.com/us-federal-tax-history-4145479.

Bird, Beverly. "IRS Audits: The Ins and Outs." The Balance, January 6, 2019. https://www.thebalance.com/overview-of-individual-taxpayer-irs-audit-4147677.

Bird, Beverly. "The Top 13 Tax Audit Triggers." The Balance, January 15, 2019. https://www.thebalance.com/top -audit-triggers-that-catch-irs-attention-4153034.

Blankley, Bethany. "Report: Since Recession, 10 States, Including Illinois, Operate at Structural Deficits." Watchdog.org, November 29, 2018. https://www .watchdog.org/national/report-since-recession-states -including-illinois-operate-at-structural-deficits/article _aa7cd58e-f34b-11e8-8794-ef3eed6d3a8c.html.

Cammenga, Janelle. "State and Local Sales Tax Rates, 2019." Tax Foundation, January 30, 2019. https://taxfoundation .org/sales-tax-rates-2019.

Caplinger, Dan. "Capital Gains Tax Rates: A Comprehensive Guide." Motley Fool, January 14, 2019. https://www .fool.com/taxes/2019/01/14/capital-gains-tax-rates-a -comprehensive-guide.aspx.

Center on Budget and Policy Priorities. "Policy Basics: Where Do Federal Tax Revenues Come From?" December 6, 2018. https://www.cbpp.org/research/federal-tax/policy -basics-where-do-federal-tax-revenues-come-from.

Center on Budget and Policy Priorities. "Policy Basics: Where Do Our Federal Tax Dollars Go?" January 29, 2019. https://www.cbpp.org/research/federal-budget/policy -basics-where-do-our-federal-tax-dollars-go.

Cerullo, Megan. "Some of America's Biggest Companies Paid Little to No Federal Income Tax in 2018." CBS News, March 4, 2019. https://www.cbsnews.com/news/2018

WHAT YOU NEED TO KNOW ABOUT TAXES

-taxes-some-of-americas-biggest-companies-paid-little
-to-no-federal-income-tax-last-year.

Daniels, Jeff. "Colorado Legal Pot Industry Sales Grew
3 Percent in 2018, Top $6 Billion Since Recreational Use
Began." CNBC, February 12, 2019. https://www.cnbc
.com/2019/02/12/colorado-pot-industry-sales-top-6
-billion-since-adult-use-began.html.

Fiorillo, Steve. "Income Tax: Definition, Brackets and State-
By-State Differences." The Street, February18, 2019.
https://www.thestreet.com/personal-finance/taxes
/what-is-income-tax-14836464.

Fox, Cynthia G. "Income Tax Records of the Civil War Years."
Prologue Magazine 18, no. 4 (Winter 1986). https://www
.archives.gov/publications/prologue/1986/winter/civil
-war-tax-records.html.

Fox, Justin. "The Mostly Forgotten Tax Increases of 1982–
1993." Bloomberg, December 15, 2017. https://www
.bloomberg.com/opinion/articles/2017-12-15/the
-mostly-forgotten-tax-increases-of-1982-1993.

Frankel, Matthew. "How Likely Is a Tax Audit?" Motley Fool,
April 23, 2018. https://www.fool.com/taxes/2018/04/23
/how-likely-is-a-tax-audit.aspx.

Gale, William G. "(Not So) Happy Birthday to the Tax Cuts
and Jobs Act." Tax Policy Center, December 19, 2018.
https://www.taxpolicycenter.org/taxvox/not-so-happy
-birthday-tax-cuts-and-jobs-act.

Goodman, Bonnie K. "OTD in History … August 13, 1981,
President Ronald Reagan Signs Biggest Tax Cuts into

Law." Medium, August 13, 2018. https://medium.com
/@BonnieKGoodman/otd-in-history-august-13-1981
-president-ronald-reagan-signs-biggest-tax-cuts-into
-law-2c782dc53670.

J.K. Lasser Tax Institute. *J.K. Lasser's Your Income Tax 2019*.
Hoboken, NJ: John Wiley & Sons, 2019.

Luscombe, Mark. "A Tax Cuts and Jobs Act Checklist for
2019." Accounting Today, December 18, 2018. https://
www.accountingtoday.com/list/a-tax-cuts-and-jobs-act
-checklist-for-2019.

Mercadante, Kevin. "Everything You Need to Know About
Filing Your 2018 Tax Returns." DoughRoller, February 13,
2019. https://www.doughroller.net/taxes/guide-to
-filing-your-tax-returns.

Moreno, Tonya. "A List of State Income Tax Rates." The
Balance, February 14, 2019. https://www.thebalance
.com/state-income-tax-rates-3193320.

Murray, Jean. "The Benefits and Drawbacks of a Value Added
Tax (VAT)." The Balance Small Business, January 25, 2019.
https://www.thebalancesmb.com/value-added-tax-pros
-and-cons-397673.

National Constitution Center. "Blame Abraham Lincoln for
the Nation's First National Income Tax." August 5, 2018.
https://constitutioncenter.org/blog/say-happy-birthday
-to-the-first-income-tax.

Reid, T. R. *A Fine Mess: A Global Quest for a Simpler, Fairer,
and More Efficient Tax System*. New York, NY: Penguin
Press, 2017.

Social Security Administration. "OASDI and SSI Program
Rates & Limits, 2019." October 2018. https://www

.ssa.gov/policy/docs/quickfacts/prog_highlights
/RatesLimits2019.html.

Tax Foundation. "Preliminary Details and Analysis of the
Tax Cuts and Jobs Act." December 18, 2017. https://
taxfoundation.org/final-tax-cuts-and-jobs-act-details
-analysis.

Tax Policy Center. "Briefing Book." 2016. https://www.
taxpolicycenter.org/briefing-book/what-breakdown-tax
-revenues-among-federal-state-and-local-governments.

United States Census Bureau. "2017 State Government Tax
Tables." March 30, 2018. https://www.census.gov/data
/tables/2017/econ/stc/2017-annual.html.

USA.gov. "How to File Your Federal Taxes." February 26, 2019.
https://www.usa.gov/file-taxes.

US Department of the Treasury. "Economics of Taxation."
December 5, 2010. https://www.treasury.gov/resource
-center/faqs/Taxes/Pages/economics.aspx.

US Government Publishing Office. "United States Code."
Retrieved May 1, 2019. https://www.govinfo.gov/app
/collection/uscode.

York, Erica. "The Economic and Distributional Impact of the
Trump Administration's Tariff Actions." Tax Foundation,
December 5, 2018. https://taxfoundation.org/trump
-tariffs-impact.

INDEX

A

adjusted gross income (AGI),
    explanation of, 2, 48, 49
ad valorem tax, 62
Airport and Airway Trust Fund, 24
Alaska, 16, 52
alcohol, 22, 54
alternative minimum tax (AMT),
    12, 45
Amazon, 21
American citizens abroad, tax
    extensions for, 39
American Revolution, 33
American Taxpayer Relief Act, 34
Arkansas, 52, 59
art, paying taxes on, 47
assessing, methods for, 11–13
audits, overview of, 34–36
aviation-related revenue, 22, 24

B

bonds, 45
Boston Tea Party, 33
budget deficit, 12, 14, 16
budget surplus, 16
Bush, George W., 34

C

California, 14, 52

capital gains tax, 47
C corporations, 20
certified public accountant (CPA), 38
Children's Health Insurance
    Program, 13
Child Tax Credit, 49
Cold War, 33
Colorado, 52, 54, 55, 59
community centers, as sources of
    free tax help, 38
consumption tax, 13, 21
corporate income taxes, 11, 12, 13,
    20–21, 22

D

deductions, explanation of, 47–49
dependents, 40, 41, 43, 45
Disability Insurance (DI), 18
due date, 39

E

Earned Income Credit (EIC), 49
Economic Growth and Tax Relief
    Reconciliation Act, 33
Economic Recovery Tax Act, 22
election financing, 8
estate tax, 12, 13, 17, 25–26, 56
excise tax, 4, 8, 13, 17, 21–24, 28, 54

F

Federal Insurance Contributions

WHAT YOU NEED TO KNOW ABOUT TAXES

ABOUT THE AUTHOR

Corona Brezina is an author who has written numerous books for young adults. Several of her previous books have also focused on government, social, and economic topics, including *Understanding Equal Rights*; *How Imports and Exports Work*; *The Fifth Amendment: Double Jeopardy, Self-Incrimination, and Due Process of Law*; and *Understanding the Federal Reserve and Monetary Policy*. She lives in Chicago, Illinois.

PHOTO CREDITS

Cover urbazon/E+/Getty Images; p. 5 Ryan R Fox/Shutterstock.com; pp. 7, 17, 28, 39 (top), 51 (top) photofriday/Shutterstock.com; pp. 8, 21, 34 Bloomberg/Getty Images; p. 9 Rob Crandall/Shutterstock.com; p. 11 B.A.E. Inc./Alamy Stock Photo; p. 15 Andrew Burton/Getty Images; p. 19 aldomurillo/E+/Getty Images; p. 23 monticello/Shutterstock.com; p. 25 Paul J. Richards/AFP/Getty Images; p. 26 littlenySTOCK/Shutterstock.com; p. 31 National Archives and Records Administration; p. 32 Official White House Photo by Pete Souza; p. 37 tab62/Shutterstock.com; p. 39 (bottom) Mario Tama/Getty Images; p. 41 Ricky Of The World/Shutterstock.com; p. 42 Rocketclips, Inc./Shutterstock.com; p. 45 RomanR/Shutterstock.com; p. 46 7th Army Training Command photo by Sgt. Christopher Stewart; p. 48 Rawpixel.com/Shutterstock.com; p. 51 (bottom) ViDi Studio/Shutterstock.com; pp. 53, 55, 60-61 Courtesy Tax Foundation; p. 57 Portland Press Herald/Getty Images

Design and Layout: Jennifer Moy; Editors: Kathy Kuhtz Campbell and Wendy Wong; Photo Researcher: Sherri Jackson